SMALL FURRY ANIMALS

Mole

SMALL FURRY ANIMALS

Mole

Ting Morris

Illustrated by Graham Rosewarne

FRANKLIN WATTS
LONDON•SYDNEY

Something is happening in the field across the road. Small mounds of earth have sprung up in the grass. The soil feels soft, and it looks as if someone has been digging here all night. But you can't see anyone, and there are no spades lying around.

4

Who can the digger be?
And where has he gone?

Turn the page and take a closer look.

5

Quick! Can you see that patch of dark, velvety fur disappearing underground? It's a mole! This tireless little animal is a champion burrower. He works alone and uses his strong front paws like shovels to dig an underground home where he hunts, eats and sleeps. Wherever you see a molehill, there's bound to be a mole tunnelling underneath.

TUNNELLING MAMMALS

Moles are mammals. A mammal has hair or fur on its body to help keep it warm. Baby mammals are fed milk from their mother's body. Human beings are mammals too. Moles lead an underground life and spend most of their time digging tunnels.

Built for building

A mole looks a bit like a barrel with stubby
little legs – the perfect shape for digging and
tunnelling. It is 9-6 centimetres long, and its
short tail is always held upright like an antenna
as it travels through its underground passages.
A mole's strong front paws work like a shovel
and pickaxe in one. Its velvety fur is soft and
shiny and can lie in any direction, so it can easily
run forwards and backwards in the tunnel.

Whiskery ways

A mole finds its way through dark tunnels by touch
and smell. Whiskers on its face and the tip of its tail
detect anything in the way and sense the tiniest
movement. With its pink, fleshy nose, the mole can
sniff out neighbours, changes in temperature and, most
importantly, its favourite meal – earthworms.

US star

The American star-nosed mole has a fringe
of 22 finger-like tentacles, or feelers, around
its nose. It uses them to sniff out its prey.

7

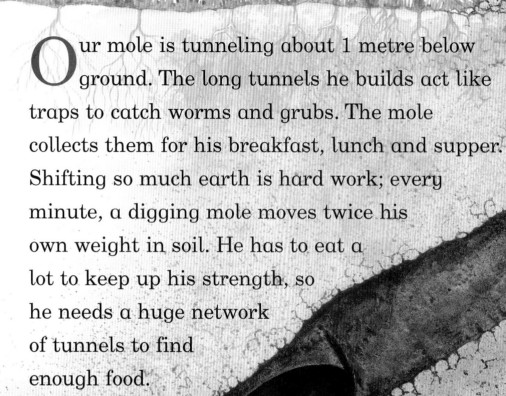

Our mole is tunneling about 1 metre below ground. The long tunnels he builds act like traps to catch worms and grubs. The mole collects them for his breakfast, lunch and supper. Shifting so much earth is hard work; every minute, a digging mole moves twice his own weight in soil. He has to eat a lot to keep up his strength, so he needs a huge network of tunnels to find enough food.

SHALLOW TUNNELS

When a mole first arrives in an area, it builds shallow tunnels that run 5-10 centimetres underground. These make ridges on the surface. It digs with a swimming motion and eats on the move. Once it knows the lie of the land, it builds a network of deeper tunnels.

Work in progress

The mole digs a straight shaft up to the surface. It then builds long tunnels one metre or more deep for trapping its prey. The mole burrows by scooping soil loose with its long, sharp claws. It pushes soil upwards with one paw, while the other paw sweeps the loose earth back along the sides and behind the itself.

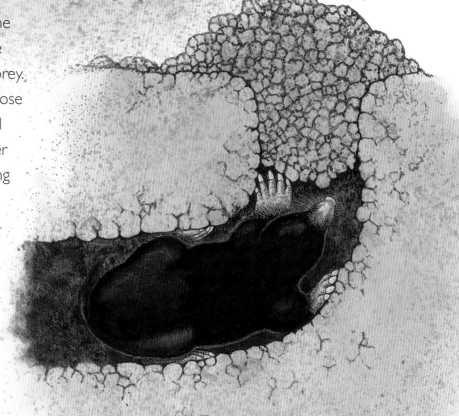

Making a molehill

The mole pushes earth to the shaft it dug earlier. Then it braces its body and feet against the shaft wall and forces the earth upwards. As the mole pushes from below, a molehill forms in the field above.

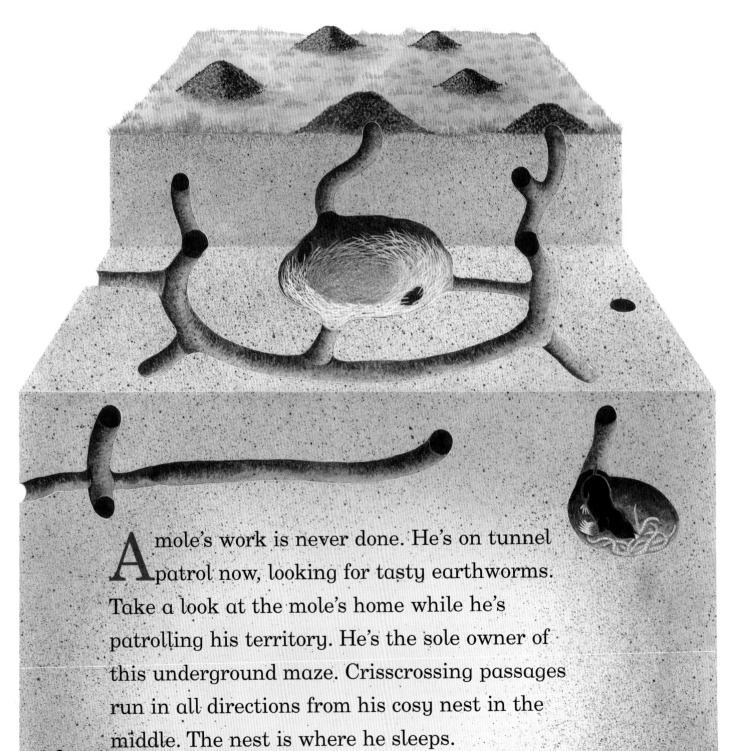

A mole's work is never done. He's on tunnel patrol now, looking for tasty earthworms. Take a look at the mole's home while he's patrolling his territory. He's the sole owner of this underground maze. Crisscrossing passages run in all directions from his cosy nest in the middle. The nest is where he sleeps.

MOLE AT HOME

A mole's home can cover an area of up to 7,000 square metres, with tunnels well over 100 metres long. Male moles have bigger territories than females. A tunnel system often lasts a lifetime and is taken over by other moles after the builder's death. (Most moles live for about three years).

The larder

A mole stocks up on food in the spring and autumn and keeps a supply of live earthworms in a special larder. To do this, the clever mole bites off the worms' heads. The worms remain alive but can't move. When it feels hungry, the mole just has to get a few worms from its own live stock.

patrolling

digging

zzzzzzzzzz

dozing

Mole patrol

A mole's time is divided between digging, resting in the nest and patrolling tunnels. While on patrol, it clears away any earth that might block its passage and fights off any small animals, such as wood mice, that might come looking for an easy meal.

The mole's tunnels are full of trapped prey, and his larders are bulging with stored earthworms, but he doesn't have running water in his underground home. So every day he takes a risky journey to get a drink. Sometimes he pops up early in the morning to lick dew from the grass, but that's very dangerous. Instead the mole has found an underground stream, and he's on his way there now. He uses one of his neighbour's tunnels to get there, and usually they don't meet.

Can you see the neighbour? Our mole can't see him, but he suddenly smells him and speeds off in another direction. That was close!

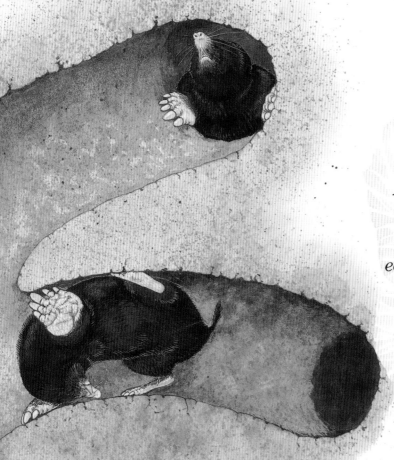

NEIGHBOURHOOD WATCH

Although moles are loners, a number of them usually live in the same area and their tunnels sometimes overlap at the edges. As if by agreement, the neighbours make sure they don't meet and use shared parts only when the tunnel is clear. Moles make a special smell to warn other moles that they are coming.

Mole's menu

In addition to worms, moles eat grubs and any earthworm cocoons they find while digging. They sometimes look for slugs above ground. Desert moles even hunt lizards on the hot sand. However, most moles prefer to eat their meals in underground safety. A 75-gram mole eats almost 50 grams of food every day.

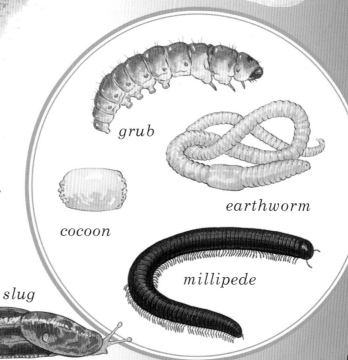

grub

earthworm

cocoon

millipede

slug

Every year in the spring, the mole goes on a long journey to find a mate. He knows a female mole's burrow, but he doesn't want to risk running into a male neighbour, especially as they are all rivals when it comes to finding mates. So he is travelling by river. He's a very good swimmer, and his digging hands make excellent paddles. Although he won't have any trouble finding the female, he'll have to be careful. Female moles can be very fierce if they are not ready to mate.

Mating

Male and female moles come together only during the short breeding season in early spring. When a female is ready to mate, she gives out a special smell. This tells the male that it is safe to approach her nest. But she'll allow a visitor into her tunnels only for two or three days, and if a male arrives at the wrong time or stays too long, there'll be a nasty fight.

Fast roads

In February, March or April, male moles may leave their territory and build a fast tunnel to find females. These tunnels, called courtship runs, are up to 5 centimetres deep and will not be used again. A mole can dig a 100-metre courtship run in one day. Male moles lose a lot of weight during their mating search because they can't hunt as much.

15

Can you see the mole next to that huge molehill? What's going on? Has the male mole got lost on his journey? No, this is his female mate, and she's coming out to collect dry leaves and grass. She will soon have babies and is preparing a warm nest for them. The male doesn't help and will never see the young. He's probably already back on tunnel patrol in his own territory.

The fortress

In areas near rivers, where there might be flooding, you might find large molehills more than 1 metre high. Each one is a mole's fortress, which is a nest surrounded by tunnels in a pyramid above the ground. The large mound of earth keeps the nest warm. In the spring, female moles often build a fortress to protect their young from drowning.

MOLE MAP

Moles know their underground territory very well. A mole can find its way back to a tunnel entrance from the other side of a stream, road or railway embankment. It's as if moles carry a picture of their tunnel system like a street map in their head.

The breeding nest

After mating, the female mole is pregnant for about four weeks. Before giving birth, she lines a nest with grass, leaves, moss and other soft materials. She makes dangerous night-time journeys above ground to collect the nest lining. The breeding nest is about the size of a football.

Four baby moles were born on this chilly April morning. They are tiny, hairless creatures, but their mother keeps them warm and feeds them with her own milk. Each baby weighs only about three grams, and the mother has to be careful not to squash her young. If you were to look through a magnifying glass, you would see that the little moles already have their parents' big shoulders and digging paws.

MOLE GROWTH NOTES

*Litter size: Usually 3 or 4, but can
be up to 7 babies
At birth: Naked and blind
  Colour: Pink
  Weight: 3-3.5 grams
At 14 days: Fur starts growing
At 22 days: Eyes open
  Weight: 40 grams
  Length: 8 centimetres
  Coat: shiny grey-black fur
At 5 weeks: Explore tunnels with mother
At 4 to 6 weeks: Stop drinking mother's
  milk and start eating solids
At 6 to 7 weeks: Start leaving mother's
  burrow and go above ground
At 9 weeks: Almost adult size*

BABY FOOD

*The mother's milk is very rich,
and the babies suck it from four
teats under her body. Young moles
grow very quickly, and their mother
feeds them five or six times a day.
During this time, the mother mole
gets little rest and has to go on
extra hunting trips to keep
up her strength.*

Teething troubles

Moles have sharp teeth which are perfect for eating insects.
Good teeth are important, and moles somehow know that
earth and grit wear them down. So before eating an
earthworm, a mole cleans its outer skin by pulling the worm
up and down between its claws and squeezing out any grit.

The young moles are on a family outing. They are five weeks old and have beautiful coats of silver-black fur. The mole toddlers eat solid food now and, like their parents, they love earthworms! Every day the mother takes the four youngsters through her tunnels, and they already know their way around. But mother mole won't allow them to stay with her for much longer. In a couple of weeks, they'll have to leave and look after themselves.

Growing up

At five weeks of age, young moles leave the nest and explore the tunnels with their mother. On these trips they start searching for their own food, but they can't dig yet. They stay with their mother for another two weeks, but then they'll have to leave home. If a young mole doesn't want to go, its mother will force it out.

HUNGRY AND COLD

Without a tunnel, young moles can't trap food. They catch what they can find, but this is usually not much. Many die shortly after leaving their mother's burrow. They may starve, freeze to death or be eaten by other animals.

Homeless

At seven weeks of age, young moles leave home or are chased away by their mother. The homeless youngsters wander about on their own. Setting up a home is difficult. The young moles may try to build a tunnel, but they don't really know how to dig. If a youngster wanders into another mole's tunnel by mistake, it is chased away at once.

21

It's a dark night and the young moles are out in the open. Can you see them? A prowling fox has spotted something moving and creeps up on the helpless young mole. Suddenly the fox pounces on its prey and snaps it up.

MOLE'S ENEMIES

Above ground, foxes, cats and dogs are mole-hunters. Owls and hawks attack from the air. That's why moles mainly stay underground and come out only when looking for nesting material or water. The weasel is the only animal that can chase a mole through its tunnels.

22

MOLE AND MAN

Farmers and gardeners don't like moles because they make molehills in fields and lawns. To keep the mole population down, people trap or poison them. However, we sometimes forget that moles can also be helpful. They eat insects that damage grass and crops, and their tunnels help keep the soil light and airy.

hawk

owl

weasel

cat

fox

Fur trimmings

Mole fur used to be very fashionable for making hats, coats and waistcoats. About a million moles were trapped every year in Britain before people started wearing fake fur and the mole's fur was no longer needed.

Who's that tunneller? Is it the mother mole? No, it's one of her lucky youngsters. She was just starting to dig her first tunnel when she stumbled into this ready-made underground home. The long tunnels were empty, and there was no smell of other moles anywhere. The larder was still stocked with worms. Perhaps the previous owner had an accident and died. The young mole is busy digging a deeper tunnel for winter hunting. Count the molehills in the field – there will soon be many more.

Giant golden mole

The giant golden mole is a distant relative of smaller moles. True to its name, this African mole is the largest of its family. It is 20-24 centimetres long and weighs up to 1.5 kilograms. Golden moles are blind but go on midnight hunts for lizards and insects above ground. It's a mystery how it finds its way back to its burrow!

MOLE NEWS

400 Worms found in mole's larder.
Half of all young moles die in their first year.
Healthy moles groom themselves after every meal.
Tunnel traps prove that sunrise is the best time for catching earthworms.

Cousins around the world

The smallest mole is the long-tailed shrew mole of China and Burma. It is just over 5 centimetres long, with a 2.5-centimetre tail.

The Russian desman, a very big mole, leads a watery life. It hunts for food in ponds and streams, using its tail as a rudder.

The star-nosed mole lives in underground tunnels but searches for food at the bottom of ponds and streams.

25

MOLE
CIRCLE OF LIFE

After mating, female moles build a breeding nest before giving birth to their young.

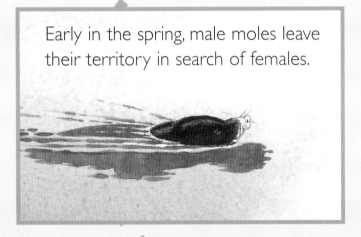

Early in the spring, male moles leave their territory in search of females.

Moles are fully grown by the end of the year.

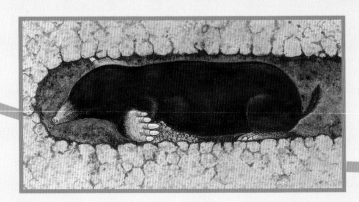

At one month of age, youngsters start exploring underground tunnels.

At 10 weeks of age, young moles start digging their own tunnels or move into empty territory.

Before they are two months old, youngsters leave their mother's burrow and go above ground.

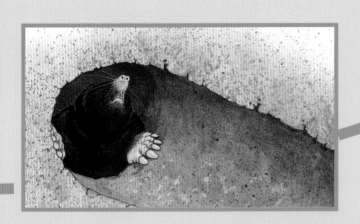

Glossary

brace To press firmly against something.

breeding nest A nest where an animal cares for its young as soon as they are born.

cocoons Silky cases that protect earthworms' eggs.

fortress A mole's nest in a pyramid-shaped mound above the ground.

grub The young form of an insect.

larder A place for storing food.

mate When a male and female animal come together to make young.

molehill A mound of earth pushed upwards by a burrowing mole.

patrol To keep watch over an area.

prey An animal that is killed and eaten by another animal.

28

ridge A narrow strip of ground that is raised higher than normal.

shaft A tunnel that goes straight down into the ground.

shallow Not very deep.

territory The area that an animal defends against animals of the same kind, to keep them away.

INDEX

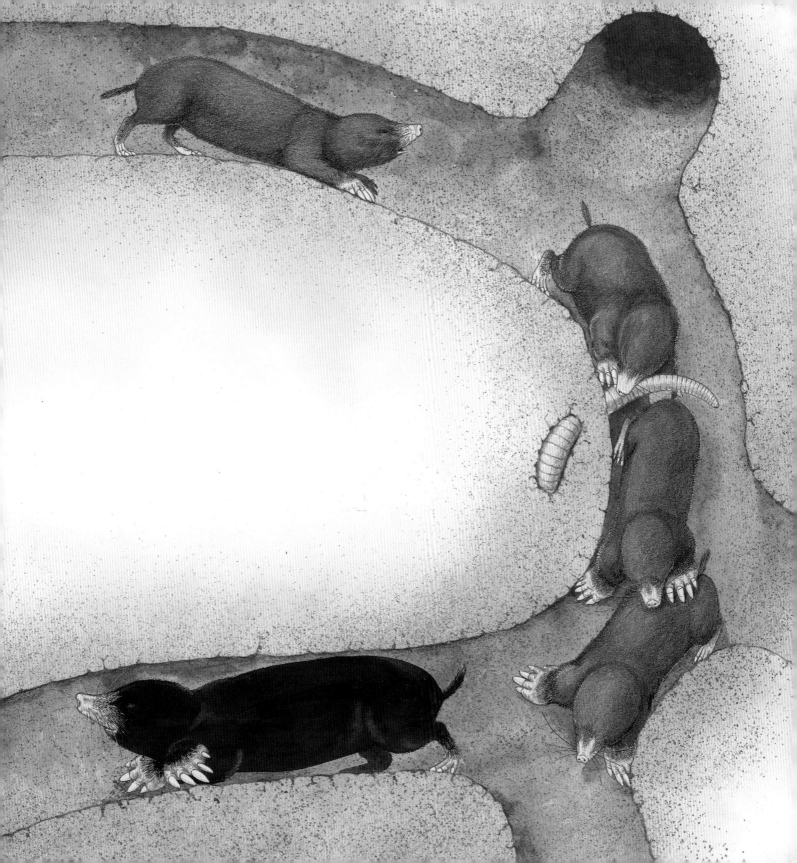

An Appleseed Editions book

First published in 2005 by Franklin Watts
96 Leonard Street, London, EC2A 4XD

Franklin Watts Australia
45-51 Huntley Street, Alexandria, NSW 2015

© 2005 Appleseed Editions

Created by Appleseed Editions Ltd,
Well House, Friars Hill, Guestling, East Sussex, TN35 4ET

Designed by Helen James
Illustrated by Graham Rosewarne

Photographs by Corbis (James de Bounevialle; Cordaiy Photo
Library Ltd., John Wilkinson; Ecoscene, Michael & Patricia Fogden),
Gary Meszaros/Dembinsky Photo Associates

ISBN 0 7496 5842 8

A CIP catalogue for this book is available from the British Library.

Printed and bound in Thailand